Ten Commandments Of

Ten Commandments Of A Down

The Way Girl

Ten Commandments Of A Down The Way Girl

Disclaimer:

This book is in no way an attempt to mock GOD or the Holy Bible. This book is an inspiration from the understanding of the world Bible to mean Basic Instructions Before Leaving Earth.

The Author makes no guarantees about the results of taking any action, whether recommended in this book or not. The Author provides educational and informational resources/advice that is intended to help readers of the book succeed in, relationships, friendships, and otherwise. You nevertheless recognize that your ultimate success or failure will be the result of your own efforts and decisions, your particular situation, and other circumstances beyond

Ten Commandments Of A Down The Way Girl

the control and/or knowledge of the Author. The Author is not a professional or relationship expert. This book should not be used as a substitute for counseling or mental health treatment. If you are experiencing mental health issues please text BRAVE to the Crisis Text Line at 741741.

© 2024 Author Katrina Moore•

Ten Commandments Of A Down The Way Girl

Table of Contents

Introduction

1. Thou Shall Love Thy Self First
2. Thou Shall Sponsor Thy Self
3. Thou Shall Not Date Potential
4. Thou Shall Not Take Care Of A Man
5. Thou Shall Not Become a Babymother
6. Thou Shall Not Chase A Man
7. Thou Shall Not Be Too Nice
8. Thou Shall Not Seek Revenge
9. Thou Shall Not Settle
10. Thou Shall Keep Going, Always

Conclusion

Ten Commandments Of A Down The Way Girl

Introduction

The other day, I was approached by a man while pumping gas. "You're too pretty to be pumping gas, your man should be doing that," he said while approaching me. I thought that pick-up line was pretty cheesy, but I entertained the conversation momentarily. We exchanged numbers, and during our first conversation, he revisited the topic of why I was single. I bluntly told him that I was single because I refuse to conform to the style of this new dating era. We talked a bit more about what my

Ten Commandments Of A Down The Way Girl

standards were and things of that nature. After that conversation, I never heard from him again. I shared this experience with my friend, who joked, "You're always scaring niggas away, you can't get a man for shit!" We laughed, and I replied, "It's not that I can't get a man, it's that a man can't get me!" And I stand on that. There are thousands of books on relationship advice, but I have yet to find one that caters to girls like me. Girls that come from my background or girls that deal with the type of men that I've have. Which is why I've created this book. I grew up "Down The Way" around a lot of boys who grew to become my family. Through them and my own mistakes, I have learned a lot about men. I will not claim that this has qualified me to be an

Ten Commandments Of A Down The Way Girl

expert on all men or relationships. It has qualified me to speak to the things that I've personally experienced or witnessed. I hope that you will use my knowledge as a reference to make better decisions and avoid making the same mistakes that I made. A lot of the situations in this book will include or revolve around men. But men will never tell you these things. Their comfortability depends on your lack of knowledge. The only way that a man will tell you these things is if you are a part of the family. They may hurt and mislead other women, but they don't want to see that happen to the women that they are close to. And that's the benefit of being a "Down The Way Girl". We get a lot of criticism, but because of our experience and our closeness to

Ten Commandments Of A Down The Way Girl

men, we have a distinctive perspective. We can give insight on situations in a way that other women can't. We understand men well because we were raised in conjunction with them. Most importantly, we are not going for anything strange. If you have never had a friend from down the way, you do now. Let me give you a tour of our minds.

Ten Commandments Of A Down The Way Girl

Ten Commandments Of A Down The Way Girl

Commandment One
Thou Shall Love Thyself

"The greatest act of self love is walking away from something that brings you pleasure because it no longer serves your highest good" -Author Katrina

When I think about some of the most enjoyable days of my life, I always think of this one guy. He was my favorite. There was never a dull moment with him. He had a great personality. He was funny. He was adventurous. And most of all, he was fun, really really fun. I shocked myself when I cut him off. Most of the times that I have left a guy was because he did something to hurt or harm me. Not him. He

Ten Commandments Of A Down The Way Girl

added so much joy to my life. Outside of me bitching for petty reasons, I can't recall any pain that he brought me. He was a great guy. But he wasn't the guy for me. He was the type of guy that couldn't tell you where he saw himself in five years. He wasn't even sure of where he might be the next day. He was the kind of guy that you knew better than to take seriously. One day I decided that I wanted to get serious about my life. I didn't want to waste anymore time playing. So I blocked him, and that was the end of our story. To date, that was one of the hardest decisions I've ever had to make. He's probably still wondering why I did it, and you might be too.

I did it out of love. Love for myself.

Ten Commandments Of A Down The Way Girl

Most people think that self-love is about bubble baths, manicures, and pedicures. Although taking care of your body and hygiene is a factor, it's not the complete picture. Loving yourself is about taking care of yourself mentally, physically, and emotionally. Take a minute to think of someone that you love a lot. Whether it be your mom, your child, or your best friend. You only want the best for them, right? If they were dealing with a sorry man, you would tell them to leave, right? If a job was too overwhelming for them, you would tell them to quit, right? If someone was trying them, you would tell them to stand their ground, right? m. Now imagine if you loved yourself the way that you love them.

Ten Commandments Of A Down The Way Girl

Imagine if the advice that you would give them in situations was the same advice that you took for yourself. That's what loving yourself is all about. To love yourself, you first have to know yourself. You have to become aware of your likes and dislikes; your strengths and your weaknesses. Once you become aware of yourself, you then have to set expectations and don't waver. When you love yourself, you have no problem getting rid of anything that doesn't contribute to your well-being, even if it's pleasurable. When you love yourself, you understand that you are worthy of everything that you desire, so you accept nothing less. When you love yourself, you do not stay in situations that threaten your livelihood. When you love yourself,

Ten Commandments Of A Down The Way Girl

you don't live to please others, you do what's best for you at all times, within reason, of course. Most importantly, when you love yourself, you don't fear being alone because you actually like the person who you spend the most time with (yourself). Ask yourself this: if you were the opposite sex, would you date yourself? If the answer is no, then you still have work to do. I put this commandment first because without self-love, you cannot successfully apply any of the other commandments. So much of our pain and suffering comes from our own inability to love ourselves first. Without self-love, you have no compass. You have no scale to measure what you will and won't tolerate. No matter how undesirable you may think you are, I can promise you that you

Ten Commandments Of A Down The Way Girl

have a lot to be loved for. Beauty is only skin deep. I have met some physically attractive people that were so ugly from within that it made them ugly all around. Likewise, I have met some people that were not the most attractive at first glance but the beauty they exude from within made them gorgeous. Today's society will make you believe that appearance is everything. That is not true. The things you hate about yourself, someone else will love, but you first have to love them yourself. Without self-love, there is no room for you to genuinely receive any other love. Love yourself first, and the rest will follow.

Ten Commandments Of A Down The Way Girl

Commandment Two
Thou Shall Sponsor Thyself

"If you give a man the power to feed you, you also give him the power to starve you." - Author Katrina

Typical parents have the "birds and the bees" talk with their children once they come of age. My mother, however, was far from typical. Instead of the birds and the bees talk, she gave us what I will call the "Pearls and the Cheese" talk. In case that I confused you, let me elaborate a bit. By definition, a pearl is a rare, beautiful, and highly-priced jewel. In slang, a pearl can refer to anything or anyone considered rare and/or valuable. By definition, cheese is a food product made using the curd of milk

Ten Commandments Of A Down The Way Girl

but in slang, it means money. In context, the "Pearls and the Cheese" was a conversation about the value of being a woman and the importance of getting "cheese" or money from men. My mother, by both word of mouth and example, instilled in me the belief that a man sharing his money was not just an incentive but a requirement. I can remember vividly her saying "Don't mess with a man that can't do anything for you!" She believed that men that didn't provide left you only with "A wet ass and a good talking about." Besides my mother, I witnessed this dynamic within our immediate family a few other times. My aunt was married to a truck driver and she was not required to work. My first cousin, more like my big sister, was a live-in girlfriend of a drug

Ten Commandments Of A Down The Way Girl

dealer. She also was not required to work. My cousin, more like my brother, moved his girlfriend in and was the sole provider in their relationship. At this time, I had never personally observed a relationship where the woman was the breadwinner. This validated my mother's teaching and subconsciously I took it in and adopted it as my own belief. My first encounter with a man (boy) I was around sixteen years old. That encounter along with every other encounter over the last ten years or so has revolved around that belief. Not exactly in a quid pro quo type of way. I would consider that prostitution. There were a few times that I met a guy that I really liked but he did not have much to offer me. Sometimes I would entertain it for the hell of it,

Ten Commandments Of A Down The Way Girl

but it never lasted long. My mother's words would eventually make their way to the forefront of my mind. My mother's teachings afforded me a life of comfort many times. Equally, it cost me just as much pain and suffering. I believe my mother meant well. She just forgot to mention one key piece. To Sponsor yourself first. I do not disavow my mother's methods. I can attest to the benefits of it. However, having a man that can "do something for you" only works if you're first able to do it for yourself. At the age of eighteen, I met a young man who met all the requirements on my mother's list. (She only had one requirement.) He was handsome, charming, and most of all willing to provide. He made life easier for me. I had a job but it wasn't paying much so he

Ten Commandments Of A Down The Way Girl

footed the bill for everything that I couldn't afford on my own. Eventually, I birthed his child. That experience was short-lived. He was arrested and had to serve a few years in Federal Prison. Life wasn't terrible but it wasn't the same. A year later I met another man. By my mother's merit, I could even say a better man. He provided at five times the rate of the previous one. Hell, he even took it up a notch by buying me things that I had not been privy to before. Life with him was great. Until he was arrested as well. The cycle continued. The next relationship dynamic was pretty much the same. Except that I was older and so were my two children. By then, I had become accustomed to certain things and I had higher amounts of bills.

Ten Commandments Of A Down The Way Girl

Soon this relationship became more detrimental than any other one. I allowed myself to become almost fully financially dependent on it. That meant that I could not afford to leave. I attempted several times. What other option did I have when rent was due in two days? I didn't have a chance to save because I only worked part of the time. And he didn't give a whole lot of extra. Most of the time it was just enough to survive. So what did I do? I took him back every time. Even when it went against everything I stood for. Even when it compromised my values. I tolerated subtle disrespect. I bit my tongue and I swallowed my pride one too many times. Over time I grew to become miserable. I wanted out! Finally, I got out but at a hell of an

Ten Commandments Of A Down The Way Girl

expense. By the time I got out of the relationship, I was a completely different woman. Not in a good way. That is what made me ditch the "Pearls and Cheese" mentality. The idea of being a housewife or stay at home girlfriend is very popular right now. Why I do believe that some women have succeeded and are truly happy in these positions, there are other women who are not. Those women never invite you in to see the downsides of being totally dependent on a man. They don't tell you that it makes you lazy. They don't share with you the bullshit that you sometimes have to tolerate behind closed doors. They don't tell you the permanent damage that it can do to your psyche long after it's over. My advice to anyone in a similar situation or

Ten Commandments Of A Down The Way Girl

has considered adopting a similar mentality is this: Sponsor yourself! Don't just seek to deal with a man who can provide. Seek to deal with a man who can add to what you are already providing for yourself. Be your own sponsor first. Because ultimately, if you give a man the power to feed you, you also give him the power to starve you.

Ten Commandments Of A Down The Way Girl

Commandment Three
Thou Shall Not Date Potential

"Potential alone is no guarantee for success." - Robert Smith

A couple of years after coming to the conclusion that the "Pearls and Cheese" mentality was not cutting it for me, I became an "independent woman." So, I wanted to try a new approach. I decided to date someone because I liked them as a person. I did not use their inability to provide for me as a factor in my decision. That was one of the dumbest decisions I've ever made. When I first began dating him, I did not fully evaluate his

Ten Commandments Of A Down The Way Girl

financial situation. I didn't feel the need to since it wasn't a factor in my decision.. That was my first mistake. My second mistake was being too empathetic. In the beginning, he seemed to be a hustler. Although it wasn't a factor in my decision, it was in my nature to notice certain things. He didn't appear to be broke. As time progressed, he started to open up more. Eventually, he told me his "story." The story of a broken dream. The story of being an abandoned child. The story of having no family support or anyone that believed in you. Essentially, a story that I could relate to. You see, I had my own story. One that was similar in nature to his. I decided to believe in him. When he moved in with me, I didn't require him to pay any of the bills at first.

Ten Commandments Of A Down The Way Girl

After all, I had them covered before he got there, right? Among other things, I learned that his license was suspended. He was in default on his student loans. Nor did he have a resume or email address. Poor baby, I thought to myself. How could someone not teach you something as simple as creating a resume? By now, my empathy had turned into sympathy. I felt sorry for him. I wanted to help him become the great man that I knew he could be. He had all the right qualities. With a little guidance, he would turn out well. Or so I thought. I made it my business to help him reach his potential. I created an email address for him. I created a resume for him. I assisted with getting a bank account open for him. I spent hours contacting the clerk of courts and DMV

Ten Commandments Of A Down The Way Girl

for him. Once those affairs were in order, I taught him my hustle of sports betting. The future for him was starting to look promising. We scored a big win on a bet, and I decided to surprise him by getting a new vehicle. Technically, it was his money because he won the bet, but because he credited me for putting him on, he let me dictate how to spend it. After a little resistance, he eventually started to collect the money from his winnings and manage them himself. He was on a winning streak for a while. Then one day he came to me with a stupid look. He had gone broke. Not from betting but from mismanaging the money he had previously won. I was disgusted! Still, I was trying to turn a new leaf when it came to men, so I gave him a loan. I could have lived with that. Until it happened again. Once again, not due to his luck, but due to his lack of money management. In an effort to balance out the financial responsibility for me, he started giving me a percentage of his winnings. The problem with that was by the time he finished borrowing from it, it equated to him contributing almost nothing. This made me start to question my own judgment. Eventually, I completely lost respect for him. With the loss of respect came the loss of interest. I didn't desire him intimately anymore. He had gone from being a man to being a child in my eyes. He needed constant support, guidance, redirection, and discipline. Consequently, he led me to realize that potential was just that, potential. It guarantees you

Ten Commandments Of A Down The Way Girl

nothing. Only the person possessing the potential has the power to reach it. No matter how bad you want something for someone, if they don't want it for themselves, your desires for them are useless. Shortly after, I told him that it was no longer working for me, and we agreed to go our separate ways.

There is a small likelihood that you could meet someone who ends up reaching their full potential with your help. However, I personally will never know. I will never date based on potential again. Since that situation, I now analyze every man as they are. When meeting a potential partner, I ask myself, "If he remains exactly the same for the entirety of our relationship, would I still want him?"

Ten Commandments Of A Down The Way Girl

If the answer is no, then I don't entertain the thought of a relationship. And neither should you. Any man you decide to get in a relationship with needs to already be "good enough." That way, chances are more likely that he will continue to get better.

Ten Commandments Of A Down The Way Girl

Ten Commandments Of A Down The Way Girl

Commandment Four
Thou Shall Not Take Care Of A Man

"The rules of survival never change. Whether you're in a jungle or you're in a relationship." -Unknown

There is a Netflix series called Squid Game. The show is about four hundred and fifty-six players who are in deep debt. They all risk their lives by playing a deadly game in hopes of winning the 45 billion dollar prize. If you lose a game, you die. If you win, you advance to the next round. During the show, you see some pacts made and some bonds created. As the game progresses, you see these same

Ten Commandments Of A Down The Way Girl

pacts and bonds broken in an attempt to survive. When it gets down to the last three players, one player kills another to increase his chances of winning. In the end, there is only one survivor, and he wins the prize.

The players in Squid Game have two things in common with the average man who lives off women: they're broke and they will do anything to survive. Speaking from experience, when you are not financially secure, your decisions are based on survival more than anything. You will do whatever it takes to survive. That is what happens when a woman takes care of a man. Any man who is financially strained enough to allow a woman to take care of him is a man in survival mode. There

Ten Commandments Of A Down The Way Girl

are situations where a man may start off stable in the relationship, but circumstances force him to depend on his woman. I am not talking about those situations. I am exclusively talking about when a man enters a relationship where the woman is the sole provider the entire time. The problem with this is that when men's finances change, their taste changes. Or it reveals itself rather. Once survival mode ends, men are more than likely not going to be attracted to the same things that they were attracted to while in survival mode. Women either, for that matter. When men are trying to survive, they choose women they need but not necessarily want. The thing about being needed is that it makes you disposable. The minute a situation changes, your

Ten Commandments Of A Down The Way Girl

assistance becomes no longer necessary. When men's finances change, it allows them to freely make decisions that are considered better for them. It also allows them to be able to attract who they really want. Even if a man decides to stay out of loyalty or obligation, it will never be right. Any wrong move and you will remind him of how you were there before all of it. In some cases, you may even feel responsible for his success. Therefore, you will never give him praise for becoming better. Why would you give him credit for what "you" did? You will hold this over his head and guilt trip him whenever he's behaving outside of your expectations. He will grow to hate you for that. Sooner or later, he will want a woman who did not

Ten Commandments Of A Down The Way Girl

witness his struggle or contribute to his success. This woman will not see him as a fixer-upper that she invested in. She will only view him from where he currently is. Which is why she will make him happier than you ever could. It is a lose-lose situation. The only way to win this game is by not playing it. Do not EVER take care of a man.

Ten Commandments Of A Down The Way Girl

Commandment Five
Thou Shall Not Become A "Babymama"

"Don't let a night of joy cause you a lifetime of pain." Esha Moe

During a conversation with my son, he shared his thoughts with me about how he felt that some things taught in school were pointless. One in particular being history. When he asked me what the point of learning history was, I struggled with a response at first. After a few minutes, I told him that it was because history repeats itself. If you are familiar with past events, you can better predict future

Ten Commandments Of A Down The Way Girl

outcomes. He accepted that answer as truth. I tried to tell someone that same thing about his father, but they refused to believe me.

When I found out I was pregnant with my son, I wasn't sure that having him was the best choice at that moment. Not only was I already a mother of one, I was young and not financially stable. After sharing my concerns with his father, he convinced me that it was something that I could handle. More importantly, he assured me that it was something that I would never have to handle alone. At the time, he was already providing support for my daughter, who was not his, so I believed him. If he was good to a child that was not his, I could only imagine how he would be with his own. Especially since it would be his first one. Six months into my pregnancy, he was arrested. He missed our son's first steps, first words, first day of school, and four birthdays. Although his absence was due to circumstances beyond his control, it did not lessen the impact. Every girl has their own reason for deciding to have a child. It doesn't make a difference whether it's planned or unplanned; if he wants you to have his child or he doesn't; if you all are in a relationship or you all had a one-night stand. If you two are not married at the time the child is conceived, there is a good chance that you will eventually become a single mother. Even if you are married, there is still a chance that you will become a single mother. But this book is not for the married, so I'm going to

Ten Commandments Of A Down The Way Girl

focus on the unmarried. Once you become a single mother, it doesn't matter how you got there, you're there. You're no better than any other single mother. It's important that I mention this because some girls think that they are "exempt." My son's father had four or five kids after my son, each by different women. Like myself, they are all single mothers now. Why? Partly because history repeats itself. The other part is largely due to the mindset. A woman could be dating a man who has a "baby mother" who strongly dislikes him and still choose to have his child without question. A woman could be dating a man who has been labeled a "deadbeat" by women before her and she will still choose to have his child, without question. A woman could be dating a man

Ten Commandments Of A Down The Way Girl

who has multiple kids with multiple women and still choose to have his child. This woman believes that she will never become the woman before her. Don't get it misunderstood, there are a lot of women who are simply bitter. There is an equal amount that has valid reasons to dislike the father of their child. Do not adapt to this mindset. Do not ignore history. You may indeed be special or different but that doesn't mean he is any different than he was before. As I stated before, once you become a single mother, it doesn't matter how you got there. Once you arrive, your fate will depend upon the decision of the father. The father can choose to be completely absent or to co-parent with you. If he decides to become absent, your burdens double. There are no

Ten Commandments Of A Down The Way Girl

legal consequences for fathers that choose to be absent. Outside of child support, there is no other enforcement. As long as he pays the child support, he will not be punished if he refuses to show up every other way. If he decides to co-parent, it will be better than being absent. Even then, co-parenting itself is an entirely separate kind of struggle. There is a chance that you could end up with the healthiest co-parenting experience ever. There is a greater chance that you could end up in a co-parenting dynamic that could ruin your life. For starters, by the time most relationships end, the two people cannot stand one another. The only thing worse than having to coexist with a person you do not like is having to coexist while having a child with a person you do

Ten Commandments Of A Down The Way Girl

not like. Not to mention if one parent does not want the other parent to move on. That will cause nothing but drama and chaos. Even in the best of the best co-parenting dynamics, the majority of the child's needs and duties of parenting will rely on the mother. Young women without kids sometimes have the impression that it's dress-up and ice cream dates. That is not the case. You have to be physically, emotionally, mentally, and financially responsible for another human being for at least eighteen years. In some cases, a child may be born with special needs, which requires twice the effort. Being a mother is a job in itself. It's an even harder job to do alone or with minimal support. Wait until you are married to have children. The risk of becoming a

Ten Commandments Of A Down The Way Girl

single parent is still possible but at a much lower rate. Children deserve happy, healthy, and not overly burdened parents. If you're reading this and you do not desire marriage then do not become a mother until you are mentally, physically, emotionally, and financially prepared to do it on your own. Also, choose who you mate with wisely. Learn all that you can about them and their family. You don't want to end up with a child by Mike because he is cute. Then years later you find your child struggling in reading. All because you never took the time to learn that Mike had an IEP and dyslexia runs in their family. (No Offense to anyone with dyslexia). I once heard someone say "women set the standards and men adjust accordingly." I

Ten Commandments Of A Down The Way Girl

couldn't agree more. Men follow women's lead. Even with Adam and Eve. Eve ate the Apple first. It's time to reset the standard. Use protection, get on birth control, or pop a Plan B. Become a wife before reproducing. If you do not desire that, make sure that you are financially, emotionally, and physically prepared to become a mother. That way if he turns out to be the opposite of what you expected you are fully equipped to be a mother on your own.

Ten Commandments Of A Down The Way Girl

Commandment Six
Thou Shall Not Chase A Man

chase

verb 1. pursue in order to catch or catch up with.

A friend and I were at a Chinese restaurant and I ran into a dude that I grew up with. We greeted one another with a hug and talked for a few minutes. After he placed his order, he went outside to wait for it to be prepared. When he walked out, my friend said, "I want him." Since he was someone that I knew, she asked me to put her down. I laughed and said okay, but really had no intentions of it. When

Ten Commandments Of A Down The Way Girl

he walked back in to get his food, she nudged me. She told me to tell him. I said no and told her to tell him herself. So she did. "Excuse me," she said while walking in his direction. They talked and exchanged a few smiles. When she returned to me, I asked what happened. She said that they not only exchanged smiles but numbers as well. A few weeks went by, and I asked her for an update. She said that he had been acting like he's scared of her. I asked her to elaborate. She explained that she initiated most of their conversations and he always had an excuse whenever she suggested that they chill together. "I think he's gay," I said in an attempt to make her feel better. She agreed, and we both laughed.

Ten Commandments Of A Down The Way Girl

At the time, neither of us fully understood the concept. We later came to accept that this is what happens when you pursue a man. When you pursue a man, you will never know if he is genuinely interested. Contrary to popular opinion, men are much nicer to the opposite sex than women. A woman will turn a man down rudely without a second thought. Whereas, men typically turn women down by providing them a reason. "I'm married." "I don't want to hurt you." "You're too good for me." "It's not you, it's me." Still, some women will persist even after the man's own objections. This forces the man to continuously turn the woman down indirectly. Missing calls. Not responding for days. Saying he's too busy. Saying he's not ready

Ten Commandments Of A Down The Way Girl

for a relationship. Men do everything they can to turn a woman down without using the actual words. The problem is, some women have a hard time comprehending. Instead of interpreting it as "He's not into me," they believe it to mean "try harder." They then go out of their way to convince him why they're a good catch. But if you're the one chasing, how can you be caught? You cannot be a good catch to a person who is not trying to catch you. That is why it is important to never pursue or chase a man. If he gives you a reason, believe the reason. Don't try to convince yourself of anything other than what he said. More importantly, don't try to change his mind.

Ten Commandments Of A Down The Way Girl

When you allow a man to pursue you, you can be sure of one thing; He thinks you are the catch. When you chase or pursue a man, it automatically makes him the catch. If you persist and manage to succeed at convincing him to enter into a relationship with you, it will be you who puts in the most effort throughout the entire relationship. In The previous chapter I said, "Women set the standard and men adjust accordingly." This applies when pursuing men. If you start off pursuing, you have already set your standard as extremely low. The man now has no standards to continually meet for you because you didn't set any to begin with. Not only should you not chase or pursue in the beginning, you should not do it at the end either. Once someone has

Ten Commandments Of A Down The Way Girl

determined that you are no longer what they want, let them go. Do not chase them. Why would you want someone who doesn't want you? You have to understand that rejection is not personal. Like in the scenario above with my friend, just because a man doesn't desire one certain woman doesn't mean he doesn't desire women at all. Just because someone doesn't want you doesn't mean you are unattractive or undesirable. I have met and turned down a lot of men that were very attractive but were not my type. We all have different tastes. I like KitKats, and my sister likes Twix. The only thing that can truly determine which one is the best is dependent upon which one of us is judging. My point is, we do not always share the same taste as others. That is okay.

Ten Commandments Of A Down The Way Girl

We also do not always keep the same taste forever. One year Mountain Dew was my favorite soda. I drank them religiously and had no desire for any other soda. Today I love Coca-Cola and I wouldn't drink Mountain Dew for anything. That doesn't mean that Mountain Dew is no longer good. Millions of other people still love it. It only means that my taste changed. The same analogy applies when a relationship ends. There are millions of other people that will choose you. Do not waste your time and energy on the one person that decides that you're not their taste anymore.

Ten Commandments Of A Down The Way Girl

Commandment Seven
Thou Shall Not Be Too Nice

"Nice guys finish last." -Leo Durocher

And so do the girls. By definition, nice means pleasant, agreeable, or satisfactory. This is not to be confused with being kind. Kind girls are generous, helpful, and considerate of other people's feelings. Nice girls are too agreeable. They lack boundaries and do not stand up for themselves.

My homeboy was dealing with two women. One I will categorize as "nice," and the other I will categorize as a "bitch." The nice girl was his girlfriend, and I guess you can say the bitch was his

Ten Commandments Of A Down The Way Girl

side woman. When his phone rang, you could tell which one was calling by his facial expression and body language. When the nice girl was calling, he would seem relaxed or calm. When the bitch was calling, he would seem either happy or stressed. I told him that I felt like the nice girl was his peace and the bitch was his stress relief. We had a conversation about this, and he agreed. Peace is a wonderful feeling. Similar in nature, but not the same as the feeling of relief after a stressful situation. This is not to say that men do not value peace. They do. This is also not to tell you to intentionally be mean or be a bitch. In fact, I encourage you to be kind. Not just to men but to everyone. What I am saying is that being his stress relief rather than being his peace simply means you do not give him peace at the expense of neglecting your own. It means there is an equal exchange of peace. It means making him work to be your peace just as much as you do to be his. The bitch caused him "stress" because he knew that at any given moment she could be calling with her concerns about something that bothered her. Men can sometimes interpret this as conflict, which may make them feel stressed. The bitch didn't mind standing up for herself. She would tell him if there was something she didn't agree with. If he did something that was unacceptable to her, there would be consequences. This kept him on his toes. He understood that there was always a chance that if he

Ten Commandments Of A Down The Way Girl

became what she no longer wanted, he could lose her. For that reason, he was forced to meet her standards whenever they encountered one another. Which is why he put in more effort not to disappoint her. The nice girl was agreeable. If he said he would be out late, she would simply reply okay, even if she had plans for a movie night. It was easy for him to disappoint her because she never made it uncomfortable for him to do so. The nice girl accepted anything because she was afraid that if she spoke up, she would lose him. You're probably wondering if he valued the bitch so much why he didn't just leave the nice girl alone. He was lazy, and the girls supplemented one another. The nice girl was his safe place. She did not require him to meet any consistent standards so there was no way he could fail. She was constantly shifting her standards to accommodate his decisions. On the other hand, he knew that if he wasn't consistently the man that the bitch required him to be, she would be out. The moment that he decides that he can meet the standards of the "bitch," he will leave the nice girl. Men are strategic. They do not risk losing what is guaranteed. Neither woman won, but I agreed with the approach of the bitch more. Though I am not against it, I do not promote the idea of being a side woman. In this situation, the bitch seemed to be the woman whose reason for not scoring him was because she was unwilling to compromise. While the "nice" girl seemed to be the woman who secured

Ten Commandments Of A Down The Way Girl

him because she was too compromising. Getting in a relationship takes you off the market. The nice girl could miss her chance to meet the right man because she's committed to the wrong man. While the bitch still has her options open.

My homeboy was indeed a piece of shit when it came to women. Don't let that distract you from the message. Being nice may appear to make him like you more at first, but eventually, it makes him respect you less. Once respect leaves, disrespect is soon to follow. Don't be a nice girl. Don't just go with the flow. Set expectations. Require that they be met. If not met, be prepared to walk away. Stand firm on your principles and values. Enforce boundaries. Say no when you have to. Voice your

Ten Commandments Of A Down The Way Girl

opinion when need be. Even if that means going against someone else's. If being true to yourself makes him want to leave then let him go. Chances are, he was never that into you to begin with.

Ten Commandments Of A Down The Way Girl

Commandment Eight
Thou Shall Not Seek Revenge

"Don't get, get back. Get the fuck on."-Author Katrina

The morning after his birthday, I woke up, and he wasn't next to me. Worry immediately rushed over me. He had gone out with his friends the night before and told me that he would be home after the club ended. Where was he? Did he get arrested or hurt? I thought to myself as I checked my phone for any missed calls or text messages. None. I dialed his number. No answer. I tried a few more times and received the same response. I got dressed and drove

Ten Commandments Of A Down The Way Girl

to his mother's house. His car wasn't there. I left there and drove to the "spot." When I saw his car, my anxiety eased up. I parked and exited my car. I knocked on the door for a moment. No response. That was strange. So I went to the window and noticed him peacefully sleeping on the sofa. I immediately grew angry. In my mind, there was only one reason you would end up at the "spot" after the club instead of at home in my bed. My first thought was to even the score. Make him pay and feel my pain, literally.

I spent twenty-two days in jail behind that day. That was the first Christmas I had spent away from my children. I cried like a grieving mother. Being isolated in a cell tends to make you think deeply.

Ten Commandments Of A Down The Way Girl

While in jail, I realized that somewhere along the way I had come to believe that my actions were always justified whenever the person caused me harm first. I was wrong, and it would be years later that I realized I had no right to play God. I have always been a believer in the idea that you reap what you sow. But in my younger years, I was impatient and very emotionally unhinged. Instead of waiting on God or karma, I wanted to take matters into my own hands. Being in jail made me realize that when you decide to dictate someone else's punishment, when you decide that you're going to give them what you feel they deserve, you quickly go from victim to villain. Regardless of how great of a person you believe yourself to be, once you seek

Ten Commandments Of A Down The Way Girl

revenge, that shift then puts you in rotation for karma as well. Ultimately, you become no better than them. Inflicting physical, mental, or emotional pain upon another because they caused you pain doesn't make it justified. It only adds you to the list of people causing pain. It doesn't matter if the revenge is violent, spiteful, or petty. It all makes you ugly. Even after I understood this concept, I struggled. I was not able to overcome it until I was told something that changed my perspective.

I had a long-distance friend. We would see each other a few times a month. One weekend I went to see him, and he said, "I've been missing you." I was a bit taken aback by this. It was not because I didn't believe him. It was because he never sent me any "I

Ten Commandments Of A Down The Way Girl

miss you" texts. I replied by saying that if he was "missing me," why did he not randomly text me and say so. He said that if he called me every time he thought about me, I would get tired of him calling. He told me that just because he felt a certain way did not mean he had to act on it. Just because he did not always put actions behind feelings didn't make them any less real. I know that sounds like some cute gaslighting bullshit but hear me out. I told him that because I openly expressed my feelings, he should do the same. The conversation ended with him saying that I was right, of course. In actuality, I was wrong. Maybe not in that situation but in the overall concept. I needed to get a hold of my feelings. My feelings dictated my every move. Especially when it

Ten Commandments Of A Down The Way Girl

came to my need to seek revenge. If I felt something was unfair, my emotions told me to make it right. I had never learned that my emotions were not meant to be the sole source of my decision-making. To some of you, this may sound like an automatic given. Trust me, it is not. Up until that point, I thought that in order to make my feelings valid, I had to act on them. I learned a valuable lesson from that conversation. I learned that just because I felt a certain way did not mean I had to act on it. Consequently, just because I chose not to put an action behind every feeling, did not make the feeling any less real. This simple awareness and shift in perspective has allowed me to respond differently to injustices. Instead of seeking revenge, I now create distance. I've learned this response to be healthier, safer, and way more effective. Denying someone the right to your life is one of your greatest uses of free will. I now let God and/or karma dictate which punishment, if any, they deem fit. It was difficult to let go of the outcome because we all like instant gratification. But believe me when I tell you that no one who has personally caused me harm has ever ended up better off as a result. On the flip side, I have never ended up better off as a result of hurting anyone else. So again, don't seek revenge. Trust the process and don't get, get back; Get the fuck on.

Ten Commandments Of A Down The Way Girl

Commandment Nine
Thou Shall Not Settle

"Don't ever settle. For a job, for a nigga, for a frontal not laid right... Nothing! If it ain't what you want, go get what you want!" LaBrena Bell

I was scrolling through Instagram one day, and I noticed that one of my high school classmates had gotten engaged. I shared the news with my sister, and she replied, "She's been putting up with his bullshit since high school, she earned that damn ring." I have not looked at their marriage the same since.

Ten Commandments Of A Down The Way Girl

Marriage, to my understanding, means that you have found the person that you want to spend the rest of your life with. When I see couples who have been together for years and are not, at minimum, engaged, I assume one of two things. The woman does not desire marriage. The man does not feel that the woman they are with is their forever person. There are some cases when neither party wants marriage. I'm not referring to them. I'm strictly talking about relationships where the woman wants to be married. I do not care what type of dating style a man has; it doesn't take five years to get to know a person. Once a man gets to know you it should not take five more years for him to decide if you are who he wants to do life with. Especially if he desires marriage. The

Ten Commandments Of A Down The Way Girl

main reason a man who desires marriage would spend a decade with a woman and not marry her is because he is still searching for his wife. If he is still searching for his wife then where does that leave you? Settling. You're settling to be a placeholder until he finds his wife. Or you're settling to become his wife after he has explored his options and realized that no one else was willing to love and accept him in the way that you did. Secretly, you will know this, and a part of you will never feel fully worthy. Why would you settle for that when you can meet a man who chooses you the first time? Why would you settle for that when you can meet a man who is sure about you right away? Why settle for that when you can meet a man who marries you

Ten Commandments Of A Down The Way Girl

swiftly because he doesn't want to risk the chance of another man having you? Why would you settle for that when even if he is not fond of marriage, the right man will change his mind for you? If marriage is what you desire, do not settle for being a long-term girlfriend or a truly devoted friend.

You can have anything you want as long as you are willing to become the person it takes to get it. If you want something, find out what is required to get it and do that or become that. This applies to any area of life. Going after what you desire is scary. The feeling of wanting something badly and never getting it is scarier. Figure out what your desires are in life. It doesn't matter if they're big or small or different from society's expectations. Don't stop

Ten Commandments Of A Down The Way Girl

pursuing them until you are either living them or you die trying to reach them.

Ten Commandments Of A Down The Way Girl

Ten Commandments Of A Down The Way Girl

Commandment Ten
Thou Shall Keep Going, Always

"A bad day doesn't cancel out a good life. Keep going" -Unknown

Early one morning, I woke up to a hard knock at my door. It grew louder as I got up to answer. When I reached the living room, I was greeted by police officers already in my home. Confused and startled, I asked what the problem was. They responded, telling me that they had received an anonymous call. The caller informed them that a fugitive was living at my address. After a few more questions, I determined that the fugitive they were referring to was my boyfriend. Moments later, I remember both my boyfriend and I being detained on the sofa. Something prompted them to do a search, and a gun was found. They ran the serial number, and the gun was traced as stolen. They asked whose gun it was. Reluctantly, my boyfriend said that it was his. My heart shattered as I watched them escort him downstairs into the police car. Shortly after, an officer informed me that they were confiscating all electronic devices in my home. He said that because the weapon came back as stolen, they needed to take the electronics. They had to ensure that none of them was stolen as well. They confiscated four flat-screen televisions, my computer, my children's

Ten Commandments Of A Down The Way Girl

Nintendo DSs, and my cell phone. The incident caused such a scene that the property manager found out. The very next day, I was given a seven-day notice to vacate. I had seven days to pack up, find a place, and come up with the funds to move. It was impossible to pull that off. Seven days later, I was forced to move myself and my two children to a place I thought I would never return: my mother's house. Two weeks prior, my life was good. I had a supportive boyfriend. I had a job that I liked. I had my own home. I had a new car. I was a semester away from graduating college with my Associate's degree in Criminal Justice. Most importantly, I was happy, and so were my children. As if my situation wasn't bad enough, shortly after, it got worse. I lost

Ten Commandments Of A Down The Way Girl

my job. I stopped going to school because I could not focus. I ended up getting arrested for a serious offense. One knock at the door had changed the entire trajectory of my life. During that time, I did not think that I would ever recover. Slowly but surely, I did. The last three years of my life have been the most productive, financially stable, and peaceful years I've had since then. It wasn't easy to get here though. There were days that I didn't know if I was coming or going. There were days I didn't get out of bed. There were days when I couldn't see the light at the end of the tunnel, and I wanted to quit. But I kept going. Still now, every day is not a good day. But I keep going.

Ten Commandments Of A Down The Way Girl

I have been through enough ups and downs in life to honestly say, besides death, there is nothing that you can't come back from. Behind every success story is a person who didn't quit. The most beautiful things take time to develop. Today may be a bad day, but a day doesn't cancel out a good life. Keep going. Tomorrow could be the day that changes your life.

Conclusion

In this book, you have learned several do's and don'ts. Some topics may have resonated with you, while others may have not. That's to be expected. Each of you is different, and everyone's goals are not the same. The key is not to let what didn't resonate with you keep you from retaining what did. Although most of the stories in the book revolve around men, many of these commandments can be equally applied to other relationships in your life. Some of you may have already experienced situations referenced in this book, and that's okay. Now that you have the knowledge, it's up to you to apply it. If you apply it correctly, you will spare

Ten Commandments Of A Down The Way Girl

yourself trouble, pain, and the embarrassment that comes with being walked all over. Living by these commandments brings both bad news and good news. The bad news is that you may lose friends and stay single longer. The good news is that you will increase your chances of finding someone who loves, honors, and respects you. The goal of the book is to educate and empower women. I truly believe that if women raise and enforce their standards, men will rise to the occasion of meeting them. And that's what we're aiming for: getting men to be better men by becoming better women. That's the theory of a "Down The Way Girl."

Ten Commandments Of A Down The Way Girl

Ten Commandments Of A Down The Way Girl

Ten Commandments Of A Down The Way Girl

Ten Commandments Of A Down The Way Girl

Ten Commandments Of A Down The Way Girl

Ten Commandments Of A Down The Way Girl

Ten Commandments Of A Down The Way Girl

Ten Commandments Of A Down The Way Girl

Ten Commandments Of A Down The Way Girl

Ten Commandments Of A Down The Way Girl

Ten Commandments Of A Down The Way Girl

Ten Commandments Of A Down The Way Girl

Ten Commandments Of A Down The Way Girl

Ten Commandments Of A Down The Way Girl

Made in the USA
Columbia, SC
21 March 2024